SMALL LAUNDRY OPERATIONS

Introduction

The Benefits of Running a Laundry

The Costs of Running a Laundry

The Chain of Productivity & Room Flow

Sorting, Washing, Drying, Folding & Packaging

Tips for Improving Laundry Productivity

INTRODUCTION

This book is to discuss small laundry operations and is based on my experience running a laundry that produces ~500,000 pounds of clean linen annually for a vacation rental business along the Oregon coast. Our laundry facility was created in 2014 after a national linen provider bought out a regional provider who was supplying our hospitality business.

The national provider told us our costs were going to double and that if we didn't like this that we should do it ourselves. We decided to do it ourselves. We invested over $300,000 in new linen and equipment. We lost tens of thousands the first few years due to our inexperience, but have since then achieved a sustainable, efficient laundry. Our costs are half what they were under the regional provider, and less than a quarter of what the national chain proposed charging us.

One of the reasons for our inexperience was that there were no good written resources for small commercial laundry operations. Everything we've learned has come from first hand experience, hospitality consultants, laundry equipment manufacturers and chemical providers. I hope this book assists you in the creation or optimization of your own small laundry operation.

- Dean McElveen

THE BENEFITS OF RUNNING A LAUNDRY

Before getting into all of the costs associated with running a laundry, I would like to list some of the many benefits of an in-house laundry.

Long-Term Cost Savings
The number one benefit of operating a laundry for us has been cost reduction. While the upfront cost of equipment and initial linens was significant ($300,000+), we estimate a savings of over $150,000 per year compared to the national linen providers bid. Over a ten-year span our business will have more than one million dollars in additional profit to show for our small laundry operation.

Cost Control
When you run a laundry operation successfully, it's almost impossible to have your cost structure double year over year like that outside vendor proposed to us in 2014. When you work with a third-party vendor, you have no idea what the true costs they incur to service you are, and negotiating fair pricing can be difficult in markets with low competition. Having an in-house laundry assures cost transparency, and good managers will

constantly work to minimize costs.

Quality Control

With our old linen provider the quality of the product was all over the place. We would have items coming in with staining or holes, and if we failed to document this we'd be charged for it. With our in-house laundry, staff checks sheets and towels as they fold them, and we can set the standard quality to whatever we like through training. Undesirable laundry is rewashed or discarded. We're also able to purchase whatever quality of linen our hearts desire.

Quicker Turnaround Time

When we ordered from our linen provider we paid a trip charge for each delivery, and were restricted to once per week pickups and deliveries because of our location away from major cities. With our own facility we constantly have linen coming and going from our main office, and we can schedule as many pickups and drop offs as we'd like elsewhere along the coast.

Credit Card Cash Back Opportunities

With all the purchases made for equipment, linen replacement, chemicals, maintenance and utilities the business owner has opportunity to earn credit card cash back. This usually ranges from 1-2% for a business credit card. At the scale of our operation this was easily over $1,000 a year in extra cash back.

Residual Value

After ten or twenty years of operating a laundry, there will be residual value in the form of real estate, used machines and old linens. Most realized residual value comes from the real estate equity this laundry helps to pay off. Excluding real estate, even if the machines and the linen lost 90% of their value there would be a residual value of ~$30,000 from these non real estate sources.

Additional Revenue Opportunities

If you own a laundry in a rural community there's always some opportunity to grow revenue by taking on outside linen. Our company has made tens of thousands by acting as either a primary servicer or an emergency servicer for competing businesses. On one occasion we even made $2,000 in profit doing 6 hours' worth of laundry for a national timeshare chain.

THE COST OF RUNNING A LAUNDRY

Evaluating Productivity

The goal of a laundry is to produce as much product as possible, and for the lowest price possible. There are many costs that go into running a commercial laundry. To name a few expenses: facility lease or mortgage payments, utility expenses, laundry equipment, maintenance, linen replacement, chemicals, insurance, and labor. Distribution is a cost as well, but varies greatly with the nature of business and has been excluded here. Our business spans over 150 miles of coastline and so distribution cost is high, but a hotel or restaurant would have very minimal distribution cost. Out of all the expenses mentioned, labor cost should always be the number one cost for a small laundry.

 As you explore the idea of a commercial laundry or attempt to optimize the one you have, its good to approximate your 'total cost per pound' for linen produced. This allows you to evaluate if you're better off washing in-house or using a linen provider.

Below is an example of how to calculate total

cost per linen pound, and extrapolate the 'cost' associated with each item produced. These costs are approximate based on our current expenses and annual production of 500,000 lbs.

Annual Expense	Price	Percentage of Total	Price / Annual Linen (500,000 lbs)	Cost per Linen Pound
Labor	$78,000	47.85 %		$0.156
Facility Mortgage	$12,000	7.36%		$0.024
Product Replacement	$35,000	21.47%		$0.07
Chemical	$3,000	1.84%		$0.006
Maintenance	$5,000	3.06%		$0.01
Utilities	$20,000	12.26%		$0.04
Laundry Equipment (20 Year Lifespan, $200,000 for equipment and install)	$10,000	6.13%		$0.02
Total Annual Exp.:	$163,000	100%	Total $/ lb :	$0.326

Article	Weight	Weight * Total Cost per Linen Pound ($0.326/lb)	Cost Per Article
Twin Sheet	1.4 lbs		$0.4564
Queen Sheet	2.2 lbs		$0.7172
King Sheet	2.8 lbs		$0.9128
14# Bath Towel	1.166 lbs		$0.3801
15# Bath Mat	1.25 lbs		$0.4075
4# Hand Towels	0.333 lbs		$0.1085
2# Wash Clothes	0.166 lbs		$0.0541

*Please note, when manufacturers say '14# Bath Towel', this means a dozen towels combined weigh 14 lbs dry.

Variable & Fixed Laundry Costs

The great thing about laundry expenses is that most expense line items are variable costs. Wages, linen replacement, chemicals, maintenance and utilities all vary based on your level of production. Fixes costs include the lease or mortgage payment, and the cost of equipment. Because of these variable expenses, the laundry upkeep is very low during off-season months we have ~6 months out of the year.

Upfront Investment Costs

The upfront cost of our laundry excluding linen purchases was around $200,000. At the start we paid $60,000 for 2 washers and 3 dryers, $45,000 for our boiler, water storage tanks and pumps, and the remainder for our labor/piping/ducts/drainage system. We had a family member head up the project who once owned a billion-dollar construction company, so labor cost was below what you might expect. We also added a cold-water storage tank to avoid upgrading our city water meter – this saved over $30,000.

Laundry equipment can last over 20 years in a facility. Because of this longevity on equipment its best to invest in equipment that will lower your number one cost – labor. If you spent an additional $100,000 on laundry equipment and it lowered your labor costs by 20%, you would break even on my additional investment within 6.5 years. After two decades you would be over $200,000 richer. Business owners shouldn't be too concerned over the upfront cost of a laundry if they're considering installing one – most vendors will give low cost loans on equipment with 5 to 10 year repayment periods - they should focus on keeping labor cost as low as possible.

Another upfront cost for a laundry is the initial product purchase. If your linen is being distributed across several cities, you'll want a minimum of 3 items for every 1 item in use at a given time, or 3 par. If your business is in one location adjacent to your laundry you can operate with less, somewhere between 2 and 3 par. Sheets will represent the majority of the initial product purchase but lasts much longer than terry and needs less replacement year-to-year

Labor Cost
Labor cost is the top expense for a small laundry. When hiring employees, a business should hire laundry attendants at or very near minimum wage. Why? This position takes less than a day to train, does not require a driver's license, and is easily managed due to having a centralized location. Laundry isn't very time-sensitive either, meaning you can hire and work with odd schedules other employers would reject. In our experience, higher laundry worker wages do not equate to an increase in productivity.

Our minimum expectation for labor productivity was 60 lbs of laundry per person per hour. With Oregon State's minimum wage at that time of $11.25, this equated to 18.9 cents per linen pound. We advertised this to staff as an extremely reasonable target equivalent to folding ~28 sheets per hour. It's a bit more difficult to achieve when you consider all the tasks an attendant has besides folding – sorting linen, loading machines, unloading machines, and packaging. When supervising, if we're concerned an employee is underperforming we have them stockpile their finished products during the day so we can approximate their performance.

A laundry has a certain 'start up' time, during which time no laundry is being folded because it hasn't made its way through the laundry system. Our machines take around 1 hour at the start of the day to produce clean laundry for folding. This start up time encourages longer shifts, and staggered shifts so that only 1 staff member is on at the start of the day. During slow times of the year we reduce our working days to stockpile materials and ensure 8 hours of linen are present for the workday. This stockpiling also prompts staff to work faster – everyone works faster when there is a big pile of material in front of them.

Product Replacement Cost
As you operate your small laundry, an ongoing expense will be product replacement. Sheets and towels can be lost due to staining, mold, theft, and wear & tear (holes, tears, rips, piling). Businesses will have product loss at different rates depending on customer and staff behavior. The laundry facility can also influence losses. If water in the facility is heavy in minerals or iron this can cause staining or greying of material. If laundry is routinely

overheated this will also diminish the lifespan of the product.

The table below gives a rough estimate of the amount of wash & dry cycles to expect out of your product based on hospitality studies and our personal experience.

Laundry Article	Lifespan (wash & dry cycles)
Sheets	210 – 260
Pillow Cases	120 – 160
Bath Towels, Bath Mats	45 – 55
Hand Towels	25 – 30
Kitchen Towels	15 – 20
Wash Clothes	8 - 12

Why do sheets last so much longer than towels? If you think about it, many customers bath right before bed. Towels get all the grime from makeup and dirt. They're also used to soak up messes like urine, beer, or blood. Sheets receive nominal staining, often exclusively from customer sweat; the average human produces more than 200 gallons of sweat a year in bed. Fitted sheets are more prone to staining compared to flat sheets due to the pressure introduced by the body.

Linen products last much longer than terry products, but terry is much cheaper. To minimize the cost of replacement product managers should always buy in bulk, and always get multiple quotes. When we first started our laundry we sourced locally from a warehouse in California and overpaid for the product. In later years we sourced product from as far out as Florida and found it competitively priced even after cross-country freight was factored in. Below are some costs (including shipping) for product we bought in 2020 to highlight the difference in cost between linen and terry:

Item	Cost
250 TC Flat Queen Sheet, 60-40 Cotton/Poly Blend	$9.68/piece
250 TC Fitted Queen Sheet, 60-40 Cotton/Poly Blend, Extra Deep Pocket	$9.36/piece
250 TC Standard Pillow Case, 60-40	$1.53/piece

Cotton/Poly Blend	
27x50" 14# Bath Towel	$3.618/piece
12x12" 1# Wash Cloth	$0.24/piece
15x25" 3# Kitchen Towel	$1.08/piece
7x7" Pot holder	$0.915/piece

Chemical Costs

One of our hospitality consultants told us we should expect to pay 1 cent or less for chemical per pound of linen produced. At the time of his visit in 2015 we were paying triple that amount, buying solid product from a publically traded chemical company. This chemical company required at least 1 million pounds of production before they would move us to a liquid product line, and we found the solid product was one of the reasons for the absurd cost. It would often get clogged resulting in lost chemical and causing the dosage to be inconsistent.

After researching chemical providers per our consultant's recommendation, we settled on a regional company called Walter E. Nelson. Walter E. Nelson provided us with liquid chemicals instead of solid product, and we instantly had cost savings and higher performance. Our liquid chemicals are bleach, detergent, and sour. Pumps deliver these chemicals directly to the washers in precise ounce-sized doses. The staff interaction with chemicals reduced from multiple times a week to one time every month or two. With our switch we saved over $6000 a year and never plan to use solid chemicals again.

Maintenance Costs
In addition to the upfront cost of the laundry, every year a business will spend money maintaining the equipment. Some of the items that require periodic replacement include pumps, valves, motor belts, and springs. On a yearly basis dryer and boiler vents should be cleaned, and dryer lent professionally removed from ducts to prevent build up and increase airflow.

Our business is in a remote location, and so any repair our maintenance team can't handle takes 3-5 days to call out a specialized service company. Even without buying material we incur a ~$200 service charge for each visit. We have found its best to have spare parts on hand to reduce service charges and limit laundry downtime. We tend to spend $4,000 - $5,000 per year on maintenance.

Utility Costs
Being in the Pacific Northwest, our laundry has some of the lowest costs for electric and water available in the US. While we haven't found ways to decrease our water expense, we have found ways to decrease our electrical cost. For our electric we're on a 'time-of-day' metering which decreases our

cost to around 4 cents per kilowatt-hour if we use the equipment during 'off-peak' hours. Depending on your state you can also purchase electricity from a third party instead of your utility company and potentially save money. We would encourage business owners to check with their utility company for these options.

THE CHAIN OF PRODUCTIVITY & ROOM FLOW

The Chain of Productivity

If you understand math, you should do well operating a small laundry. Every laundry is composed of several processes that take differing amounts of time to complete. Each stage can be seen as a 'link' individually, and they form what can be called a 'Chain of Productivity' when combined. Linen begins the chain of productivity dirty, completing tasks in each link before moving onto the next link. Eventually, the chain of productivity transforms dirty linen into clean linen.

The slowest link in your chain dictates the maximum rate of production for your entire laundry system.

For every task in your chain of productivity, there is a mechanical input from your equipment and a labor input from your staff. Whichever input takes the most time to perform can be seen as your 'limiter' in that stage of the process – you will never complete the link faster than this time, and realistically might have an additional 10 minutes on top of this time because workers aren't perfect. Below is a table giving input time examples for each link in our laundry when we do a load of towels:

Activity (for a 90# towel load)	Mech. Input	Mech. Time	Labor Input	Labor Time	Limiter
1. Sorting	Releasing drawstrings on bags	~60 seconds	Dumping out material, sorting material	~4 minutes	Labor
2. Washing	Washer cycle to completion	36 minutes	Loading & unloading linen	~3 minutes	Mechanical
3. Drying	Dryer cycle to completion	44 minutes	Loading & unloading linen	~3 minutes	Mechanical
4. Folding	Wheeling of linen basket	~5 seconds	Picking up linen, folding linen, stacking linen	~20 minutes	Labor
5. Packaging	Cutting excess plastic with scissors	~5 seconds	Filling plastic bag with linen, tying bag, labeling bag	~12 minutes	Labor

In the above table, the slowest link in our chain is Drying (please note W & D machine times should be in sync in an ideal setup). If we had 50 staff members and operated the laundry like a Nascar pit crew, we would never produce more than 1 load of towels every 50 minutes with the equipment in question because each stage must be completed before moving onto the next link in the chain.

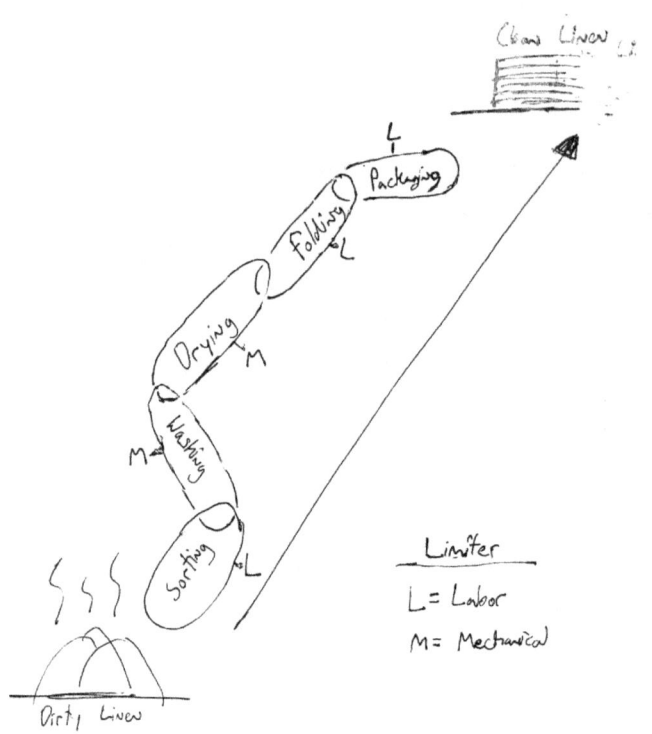

When I learned that my dryer was the limiting factor on laundry production I had two realizations. First, I realized that my laundry would never produce more than X pounds of clean linen per hour as dictated by the slowest link in my chain and the amount of machines I was using. Second, I realized that if I wanted an average labor cost per linen pound of Y, I had to staff Z employees such that:

$$Y \text{ Labor Cost per linen lb} = \frac{Z \text{ Staff members} * (\text{Hourly Wage})}{X \text{ pounds of clean linen per hour}}$$

At the time of these realizations, we were overstaffed based on the amount of linen we could produce hourly. We had a manager working the laundry that wanted to do things **their way**. They would tell staff members to 'slow down' if they were folding fast, or order them to fold in a particular way regardless of the end fold coming out the same. Our goal back then was 18 cents labor spending per pound before we made adjustments, and we were consistently landing in the 20's (did I mention our inexperience cost us money starting out?). We right-sized the operation by introducing a limit on how many staff members worked per shift, and also removed the manager. We experienced labor savings immediately with no reduction in productivity. The manager position was also removed, and consolidated in another management position job description since actual management only took ~15 minutes per day.

Laundry Room Flow
Besides the Chain of Productivity and the time it

takes to complete each link, we also observed that there is a certain time required to switch from one task to the next. This time is influenced by the physical set up of the room. If you were a worker who wanted to LOOK busy without actually being productive, you would want to have every future task in the chain on the opposite end of the room. If instead you were a manager who wanted to maximize productivity, you would want each task to be as close to the last task as possible. The next two pages highlight good room flow and bad room flow.

SMALL LAUNDRY OPERATIONS

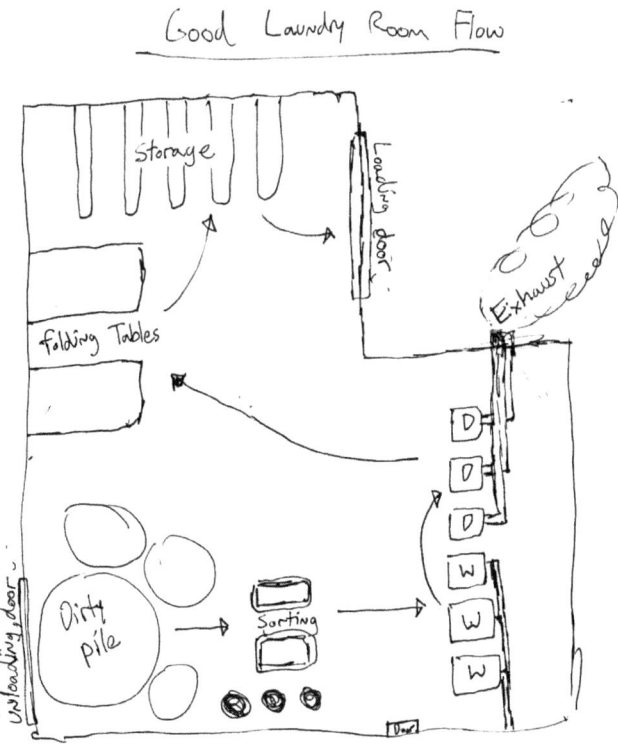

Good Laundry Room Flow

Bad Laundry Room Flow

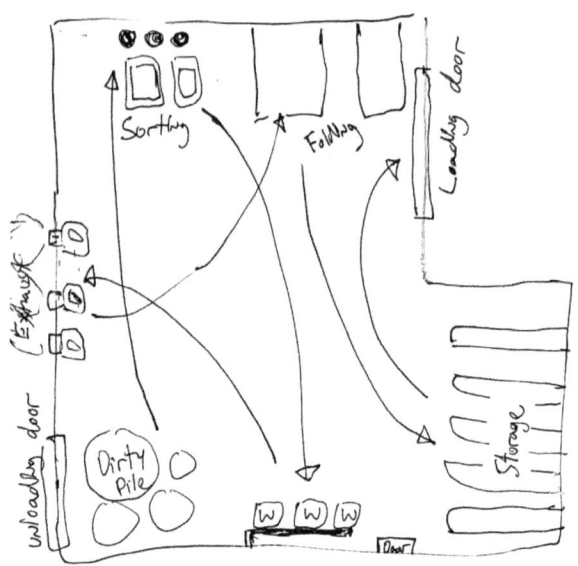

SORTING, WASHING, DRYING, FOLDING & PACKAGING

In this chapter we will talk about each phase of our chain of productivity in detail. To clean dirty linen you have to sort, wash, dry, fold and package in this order. As the laborer you should always spend **as much time doing one activity before moving onto the next**. Laborers who rapidly change tasks may look busy, but their productivity is low. The same applies for almost any work, whether its laundry or deskwork.

The Sorting
Laundry workers should always sort materials prior to the wash because different material washes and dries differently. A load of towels takes 36 minutes to wash and 44 minutes to dry in my laundry, whereas a load of sheets takes 30 minutes to wash and 35 minutes to dry. If I had a mixed load of sheets and towels I could go through the washer stage using the longer cycle, but when it came to the dryer stage a long dry time would mean scorched sheets and a short dry time would mean damp towels. This would hidden production and disrupt our goal of

efficiency.

In general, material that is less absorbent will dry faster because it retains less water. Material that is less stained will wash faster because it requires less agitation. Pieces that are smaller will wash and dry faster because they agitate easier in the washer and receive better airflow in the dryer. Pillowcases tend to process faster than any other material because of the size of the article and the nature of the fabric.

Sorting

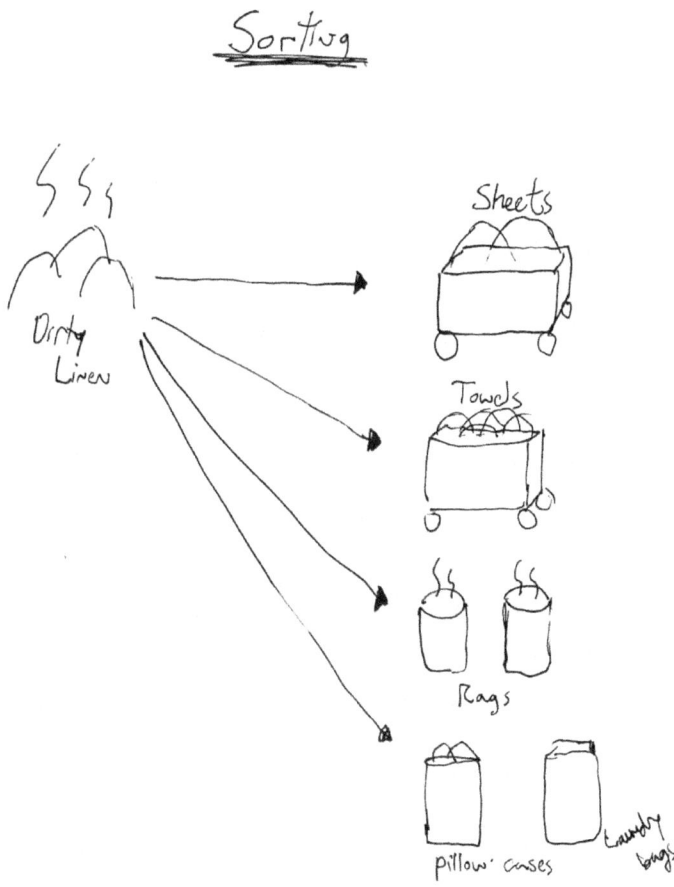

When we sort in our laundry we separate out sheets (twin/queen/king), towels (bath towels/hand towels/wash clothes/bath mats/ kitchen towels / hot pads), pillowcases, microfiber rags, cotton rags, and laundry bags into separate carts or bins. All material groups wash differently, and the latter three groups are done in residential washer and dryers mainly due to load size. We avoid washing the laundry bags in the commercial washers due to their tendency to knot during the spin cycles.

The Washing

Once material is sorted the washing stage can begin. The first step of the washing process is to load the washer. A staff member should load the washer with one material type until there is a cavity about the size of a football at the top of the washer drum. If done right, once the washer is started you can confirm a proper fill during a washer pause. Commercial washers usually pause every 60 to 90 seconds to help prevent knotting and to ensure all material is washed evenly. When a washer is properly filled you should see material fill to a level of 10 and 2 if you imagine the washer as a clock face. When washers are under-filled, linen will 'swim' in the washer and the linen will receive less agitation because it isn't forced to hit the washer drum. When washers are over-filled, the material will be unable to move freely and the center of the mass will never get cleaned.

For washer programs, we recommend you defer to the manufacturers user manual for a baseline sheet program, towel program, and rewash program. From the initial sheet and towel programs, you want to reduce the program run time as much as possible while still getting an acceptable product out. Your chemical provider can tell you how much time you have to budget to allow the chemicals to sanitize, and this time must be included in every program. Beyond the sanitizing time, there is additional time in each cycle to remove or reduce staining. If your laundry is consistently lightly soiled you may get away with a 25-minute wash cycle for sheets compared to linen with heavy soiling that might need a 40-minute cycle. This fine-tuning requires experimentation to find an acceptable level of agitation for your average product soiling.

In addition to these three programs (sheet/towel/rewash) you also want to program a rinse cycle that is used exclusively for new product. The rinse cycle should include three fills, three drains, and one spin cycle. The purpose of this cycle is to remove any chemical present on newly purchased product. Linen manufacturers sometimes coat product with chemical to reduce the chance that pests ruining the material during shipment. Rinse cycles should last no more than 15 minutes.

One thing to keep in mind when adjusting programmed times is the time expense of a washer fill and drain. A washing machine may have a sheet cycle programmed at 30 minutes, but in reality the cycle might take ~37 minutes to complete. Why? The programming on the washer does not account for the time to fill the machine with water or drain it of water, and depending on your programming this may occur 3 or 4 times in one wash. Time your washer with a stop wash and you'll find the actual time it takes to complete one cycle. You can't do much to change the drain time on the washer, but the pressure in your water pipes and your programmed temperature both influence the fill time. If you want fast fills you should use 'warm' water as much as possible and avoid 'hot' or 'cold' temperatures. The washer will fill faster because it's filling with all water connections instead of just the hot connections or cold connections.

The only time you should use 'hot' water fills is when the staining warrants it. If your stains are heavy in fat, makeup or oil a hot fill can emulsify these stains and eliminate them faster. Emulsifying means that you're liquefying the stain residue, and having it release from the material. Theoretically if you had no chemicals but unlimited hot water and time, you would still be able to clean a rag covered in grease. To emulsify stains, water temperature must be above 130 degrees. The higher your water temperature the better your results will be when emulsifying.

The last item I wanted to mention on the washing phase is the spin cycle. During the spin cycle your machine rotates material to wring water out of it, and this process decreases dry time immensely. The faster the washer spins the faster the material will dry in the next stage. Most machines will eliminate all the water their rotate speed allows for within the first 4 minutes of a spin cycle, and I wouldn't recommend having a spin cycle longer than 4 minutes. Soft mount washers offer the fastest RPM's available on the market, with some machines rotating over 400 times per minute. This high rotation speed reduces your dry time. Unfortunately, our washers have 200 RPM spins and so our dry times are longer than desirable.

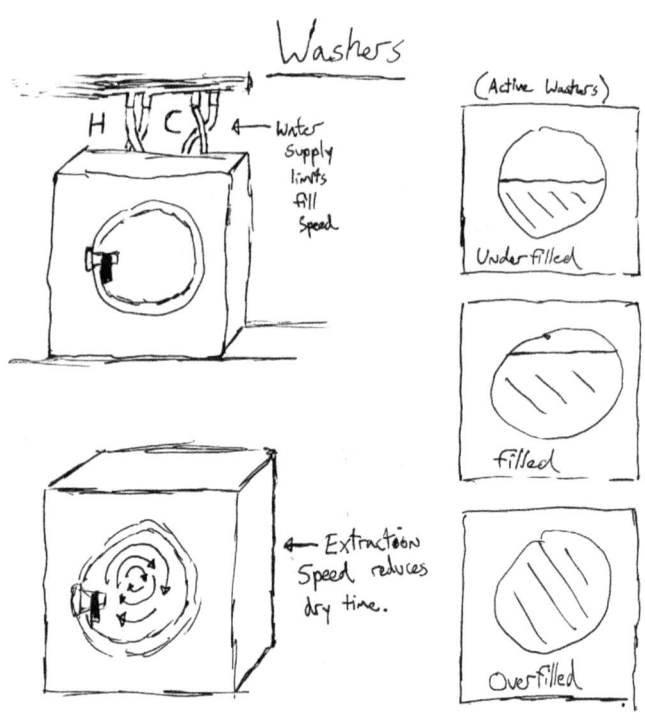

The Drying
Following the washing stage you should have a

clean, damp product. The first step in the drying stage is to load the machine. Just like the washer stage, you want to fill the dryer with a uniform material (sheets, towels, pillowcases, etc), and the amount of linen you fill the dryer with will have a huge impact on performance. If you under-fill, the material will 'swim' around the dryer drum, and can take up to 4 times the normal length of time to dry. If you over-fill, you'll scorch any material touching the dryer drum and the middle of the material won't dry. To fill a dryer perfectly you'll find wet material is usually at a level of 9 and 3 when wet if you imagine the dryer drum as a clock face. You can confirm you properly filled the dryer once it is started. A properly filled dryer will look like a constant waterfall of material once it's rotating.

Many people think that heat is what causes dryers to dry. This is not the case – heat is a byproduct and a secondary source of drying. The main source of drying comes from airflow, and the heat from the machine creates this airflow. To maximize airflow you want staff to constantly check lint filters on the dryer, cleaning them every 2 to 3 cycles when washing existing product, or every single cycle when processing new product. You also want to make sure the room has adequate ventilation to provide makeup air for your machines. Your machines use makeup air to operate, and without a steady steam of airflow the machine will not perform properly. Your dryer owner's manual will outline makeup air requirements. Lastly, you want to make sure you have properly sized dryer ducts to expel exhaust with ease. Being deficient in any of these areas can result in longer dry times.

Another common belief people hold is that when material comes out of the dryer it should be HOT. This stems from the thought that heat is the main drying force. Hot linen coming out is bad and decreases the life of your material. In an ideal world when laundry comes out it is at room temperature. Anything less and you have damp material. Anything more and you begin to burn the material, producing more lint and causing issues with the material. You will also have higher utility bills from machines running longer than they need to.

When selecting dryers, there are options for dryers with moisture sensing technology to prevent over drying. Most dryers will also feature reverse cycling options where the drum changes direction every 2 to 5 minutes to prevent knotting or bunching of the material. Some large dryers can also come with the option for lift-assisted emptying, where the dryer tips to aid in the removal of linen. We feel lift-assisted emptying is not worth the cost for the labor savings in a small commercial laundry. When buying new washers and dryers you should always size your dryers at a larger capacity than your washers so that their wash and dry times will be in-sync. Speaking with a product specialist they can recommend which machines stay in-tune best. I've been told a dryer must always be 50% greater than a washer, but I don't believe this is the case if you have extremely high RPMs anymore. In-sync machines will greatly improve the overall productivity of your laundry.

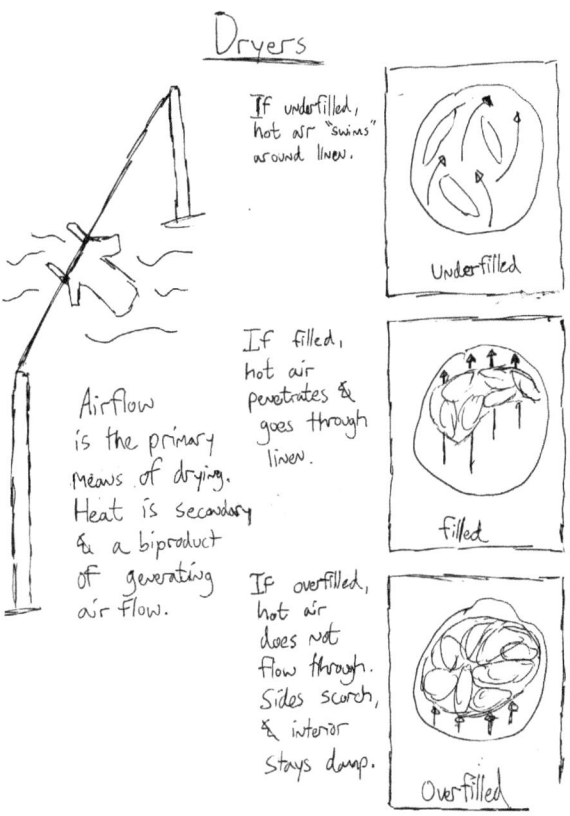

Folding

After the laundry comes out of the dryer, the laborer should fill a large bin with the clean and dried material. Just like in the washing and drying process, material should be uniform (sheets, towels, pillowcases, etc). We position our folding stations so they're within 10 feet of the dryers, and easily accessible to begin folding the material as soon as its ready.

The ideal folding environment will feature large tables with excessive surface space, and padded standing areas to reduce worker fatigue. Our tables are a little larger than a standard sheet of plywood (4'x8'), and are on wheels so we can reconfigure the room on a whim whenever we feel like. With our large tables laborers can process 3 towel loads from a 120 lb dryer before needing to package the items – more if the loads are sheets. This allows the worker to consistently fold for an hour or more before needing to package, and this makes the worker much more productive.

When we fold terry and pillowcases we keep our folds to a minimal. We fold bath towels and pillowcases twice lengthwise, hand towels and kitchen towels once lengthwise, bath mats once lengthwise and once width wise, and the rest of the material we lay flat (wash clothes & pot holders). After these folds we stack in material specific piles up to 3 feet high, and stack everything close together to prevent stacks from falling over.

When it comes to folding the sheets, we use a cheap machine called a 'third arm' or what our consultant would refer to as the 'one armed bandit'. It lets the user hold the sheet in certain positions so they don't need teamwork to accomplish the task. Its disputable if a third arm improves productivity or not – our consultant discouraged it and insisted we would be more productive folding in teams. In practice we found the third arms were more effective for us, but this may have been because we had been using it for several months before testing the folding team concept. There is one great benefit of a folding arm though – if you only fold in teams a single-person shift would only ever produce towels. With a folding arm you have more options during a one-person shift.

As staff folds the laundry, eyes should be scanning the material for any obvious stains, holes or tears. Undesirable articles should be put aside in a 'rewash' bin to be addressed at a later date. If the issue with the article is a stain, a 'rewash' cycle can be run in the washer stage to get out tough stains. If the issue with the article is a hole or tear, this usually means the item will be discarded. We like to keep track of all discarded material to have some sense of the losses we're experiencing that will eventually need replacement. In this tally we include holes, tears and stains that cannot be lifted. We recommend donating these materials to animal shelters or other charitable organizations that can make good use of them – often material that is undesirable for us can be reclaimed for non-hospitality purposes. Common rewash percentages hover between 1 and 2%. If you're getting 10% rewash something is wrong!

Packaging

After product has been folded we move to package and store it to complete the laundry process. At our laundry we store all material in plastic bags that are easy to transport because our cleaners work at hundreds of locations across hundreds of miles. The amounts we bag are included in the table below:

Article	Fold Type	Amount per Bag
Bath Towel	2 Lengthwise folds	10

Pillowcases (regular, king)	2 Lengthwise folds	40
Hand Towels	1 Lengthwise fold	20
Kitchen Towels	1 Lengthwise fold	20
Wash Clothes	0 Folds, laying flat	40
Pot Holders	0 Folds, laying flat	40
King Sheet Sets	Varies	10
Queen Sheet Sets	Varies	10
Twin Sheet Sets	Varies	20

We use 3 different trash liner bag sizes when we package. We twist-tie these bags, and cut the remaining material so that only a hand hold remains. We find for bath towels and sheet sets that a bag size around 60 gallons works well. We use a ~32-gallon bag for the bath mats, and a 10–12 gallon bag for all the other material.

TIPS FOR IMPROVING LAUNDRY PRODUCTIVITY

Labor Projections

Having the right amount of labor on during the right days of the week can greatly improve your laundry productivity. If your laundry is servicing a hospitality operation, you'll have weeks or months of advanced notice on how much laundry will be coming in. In our vacation rental business, we found that the average departure generated around 45 lbs of product. Using this average, we know how the labor will ebb and flow weekly (and even daily) months ahead of time. We would project reservations per week, and then project labor needed based on our minimum acceptable production rate of 60 lbs per labor hour. Below is an example table showing the weekly calculations. You can also break this down by day if you're unsure on the best days of the week to staff!

Week Range	Projected Reservations	Average linens lbs (based on 45 lbs per res average)	Labor Hours (based on 60 lbs per labor hour)
May 1–7	140	6,300	105
May 8–14	180	8,100	135
May 15 - 21	220	9,900	165
May 22 - 28	150	6,750	112.5

Averaging linen produced by vacation rentals can be a bit tricky as individual one checkout can represent a studio unit or a 7 bedroom+ home. I based my average number on departure behavior during high-season as I know every single unit will have at least one departure per week. For a hotel or motel business, creating an average linen figure will be much easier.

Improving Worker Quality of Life
Earlier in this text I outlined why I felt this position

should be priced at or near minimum wage. That being said, everyone should want happy workers! Things we did to improve the work environment included; buying anti-fatigue standing mats, installing a large fan for hot summer days, allowing drinks in the work space, allowing music in the workplace (both headphones and stereos), being flexible with launch hours, time off requests and part-time schedules, and supplying snacks and drinks throughout high-season months. We were okay with hiring someone who only wanted to work a day or two a week, or if they only wanted to work the nightshift after their other job let out. Many workers (myself included!) love to diversify their income, but usually do not have time for a full-time position. Part-time labor is the best.

Supply Sourcing

Our business prides itself on being cheap (frugal!). We've shopped several product suppliers and the lowest cost linen provider we've found independently so far in the US is 'Hospitality Depot' out of Florida. When we joined a hospitality buying group (*Avendra*), our prices found independently could not compete with the average price savings we found as part of the buying group. We now buy linens, soaps, shampoos, trash bags, paper products and more through this group. There are purchase restrictions related to the relationship, but if you have size and a desire to save money, I encourage you to explore becoming part of a hospitality buying group!

Servicing Outside Clients

Once you become established and can gauge your cost per linen pound, you can go out and bid on business to reduce your fixed costs! You'll know what type of profit margin you'll have based on what you can get someone to agree to. One thing I recommend when you seek out clients is that you always have a NOG policy (Not Our Goods!). You do not want to be supplying linen as it's expensive and hard to scale clientele without putting big investments in. When I went to outside clients I required that they supply the laundry, and shot for a minimum of 20% profit margins. If they wanted emergency services, for instance their laundry was down due to major equipment failure, I would shoot for 75%+ profit margins. Laundries are expensive and it's great to reduce those fixed costs!

Building in Redundancy

If you are just starting a laundry, redundancy is important to keep in mind. If you're really small you might only have a 60 or 100 lb washer. A big risk you have with a small laundry is that you only have one washer or one dryer, and it fails during your busiest week of the year! As you build, keep redundancy in mind. Two washers are better than one, and three washers are better than two! I've seen motherboard replacements take two weeks, and without built-in redundancy my guests would not have had sheets.

Sometimes it's better to have more capacity than you need, and you should consider this if you have a small laundry.

Getting Rid of Packaging

If your cleaners pull linen from the same facility that your laundry is at, consider doing away with packaging. Business owners can buy linen carts on wheels that can hold dozens and dozens of towels or sheets. With any laundry, the goal is to produce linen as fast as possible. Some might worry about if it is sterile or not, but I've seen laundry carts used in a hospital laundry in Roseburg so if they're doing it you should have no worries! If you can skip or reduce the packaging step of a laundry using carts I highly recommend it!

ABOUT THE AUTHOR

Dean Mcelveen

Born in 1992, Dean McElveen has a bachelor's degree in math with a background in engineering from the University of Washington. Upon graduating, he worked for several years in the vacation rental hospitality industry along the Oregon coast. He currently works remotely for a vacation rental business on the east coast, and is enjoying time with his significant other and their 12 children.... Just kidding, it's still 2, but he's working on it!